The Kresge Eminent Artist Award celebrates
an exceptional artist in the visual, performing
or literary arts for lifelong professional
achievements and dedication to metropolitan
Detroit's cultural community.

Marie Woo is the 2020 Kresge Eminent Artist.

This monograph celebrates her life and work.

WONDER AND FLOW

Marie Woo
2020 KRESGE EMINENT ARTIST

WONDER AND FLOW

Nichole Christian, editor
Patrick Barber, art director

With contributions from
Mary Barringer
Leslie Raymond
Tom Phardel
Steve McBride
Margaret Carney, PhD

THE KRESGE FOUNDATION

Table of Contents

6   **FOREWORD**   RIP RAPSON

9   **ARTIST'S STATEMENT**

10   **Freely Marie**
How Marie Woo redefined ceramic
excellence and creative ease
NICHOLE CHRISTIAN

36   **Marks on Many**
Select voices on Marie Woo's
ceramic journey

38   **Spark from Afar**
Woo's wondrous influence on
other women makers
MARY BARRINGER

43   **Marie Undivided**
The maker and mother as one
LESLIE RAYMOND

48   **Bonds in Clay**
A mission to make clay matter
TOM PHARDEL

52   **Full Circle**
Woo's roots as an educator revisited
STEVE MCBRIDE

57   **Persistent Preservationist**
A journey beyond the wheel
MARGARET CARNEY, PHD

62   **In Harmony**
Selected works

92   **The Spirit of
Chinese Pottery**
A reprint of an essay from
Studio Potter magazine
MARIE WOO

100   **SELECT WORKS, PROJECTS & AWARDS**

104   **OUR CONGRATULATIONS**

106   **THE KRESGE EMINENT ARTIST AWARD
AND WINNERS**

110   **INDEX**

Foreword

IT BEGINS WITH THE TOUCH — hands on spinning clay, shaping, creating first a cylinder and soon something uniquely Marie Woo's.

Glazed and fired, perhaps weathered outdoors, the destiny of an anonymous chunk of clay in Marie's possession is as much a mystery to her as it is to us. Perhaps it will become a recognizable pot, or a post-pot object that we recognize only as a piece of sculpture. What we call it is less important than what it does. It will now touch us wherever, whenever we encounter it, in a photograph or, all the better, close up. It will touch us the way glazed clay creations have endured centuries and thousands of miles to touch Marie and help mold her aesthetic.

That ability to cross, to transcend, time and space, cultures and geography is one of the defining attributes of art — the greater the transcendence, the greater the art. We've seen it in each of our 11 previous Kresge Eminent Artists, and we see it again in our 2020 Eminent Artist, Marie Woo.

The first ceramicist honored as a Kresge Eminent Artist, Marie is a practitioner, a scholar, a curator and a teacher. She is both a preservationist steeped in old-school traditions and an experimentalist expanding the tradition. In her 70-year career, she has been an inspiration to her peers and a role model for younger artists finding their way. She is internationally renowned, and we have benefited in numerous ways from the fact that Southeast Michigan has been her home for five decades.

The arc of her story is here: her upbringing in a family dedicated to education but oblivious to art, her encounter with a grade-school teacher who encouraged her expressive spark, subsequent teachers who nourished her talent, the wanderlust that took her to southeast Asia, the confluence of influences and intuitions that she effortlessly calls on when she is in — as she puts it — "dialogue" with clay.

Our hope is that in this year of social distancing and its discontents we can listen in on that dialogue and learn something useful. We might all take inspiration from Marie Woo and her humble dedication to work that can dissolve time and distance to touch us.

RIP RAPSON

PRESIDENT AND CEO

THE KRESGE FOUNDATION

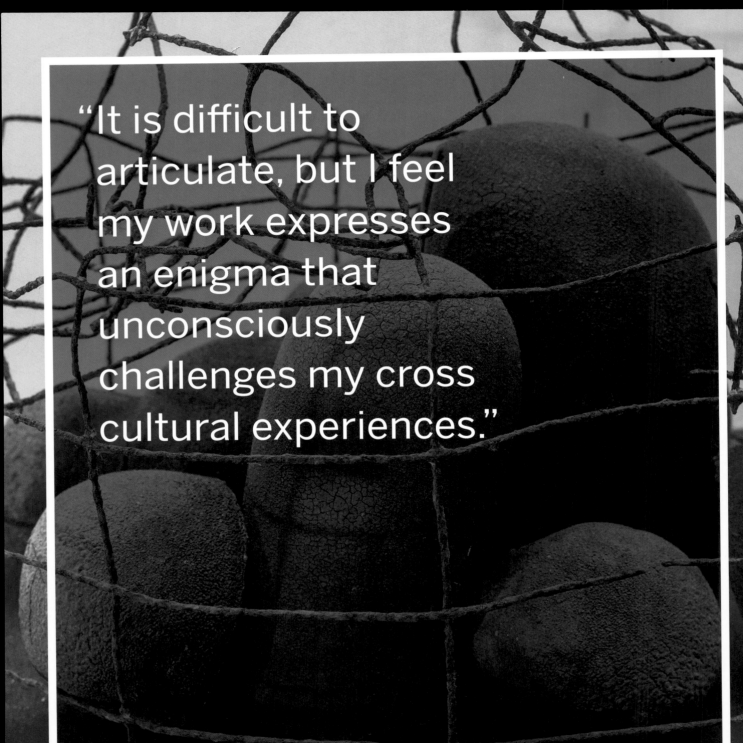

"It is difficult to articulate, but I feel my work expresses an enigma that unconsciously challenges my cross cultural experiences."

Artist's Statement

Ways of Woo

It is not easy to talk about explorations in search of aesthetic concepts. There is a permanence of ideas and forms when clay is frozen by fire. But unfired clay forms, when exposed to the natural elements, become slowly transformed, reclaimed and absorbed back to the earth, a metaphor for life. Ideas and built forms are erased and no longer recognizable.

I believe in time there comes a balanced harmony nurtured by all the rich nutrients of intimate experiences, by gathering the essence while separating and discarding the irrelevant, and extraneous.

Then ideas evolve and come to life, and occasionally they might become art.

MARIE WOO

2020

How Marie Woo redefined
ceramic excellence
and creative ease

Nichole Christian

FREELY
MARIE

True perfection seems imperfect,
yet it is perfectly itself.
LAO-TZU, *TAO TE CHING*

There are lots of things to see,
unwrapped gifts
and free surprise.
ANNIE DILLARD, *THE ABUNDANCE*

TO ENTER THE WORLD of Marie Woo one must be patient, willing to wonder and wait as she does for ideas, concepts and life experiences to mix and comingle into form, into being.

This is Woo's way.

This is how she's shaped an abiding fidelity to the ineffable qualities of clay into a near seven-decade career that has earned her accolades from around the world. Woo's creations — pots, bowls, elegant circular sculptural objects, and wall pieces — are so fiercely guided by intuition that most defy description, including her own. Some say there is a spirit, or at least a spiritual feeling, alive in her touch, a transmission of vitality hidden in her fingers sent straight from her heart.

"I'm terrible with words," says 92-year-old Woo. She chuckles then tries again. "I can't express it so easily in a description, but I think unconsciously I just try to have this dialogue with the clay," she says, her voice a beguiling mix of inner calm and easy, frequent, laughter. "I try to make a balance of harmony with the material, with nature, yin and yang. But it's like Tao; if you try to explain it, it's not Tao. It's a process that just evolves."

The evolution of Marie Woo is most surprising to Marie Woo.

She is a lifelong artist who insists "I never thought of making a lifetime of work. I just kept my hands in the clay. Everything is an experiment." Yet few

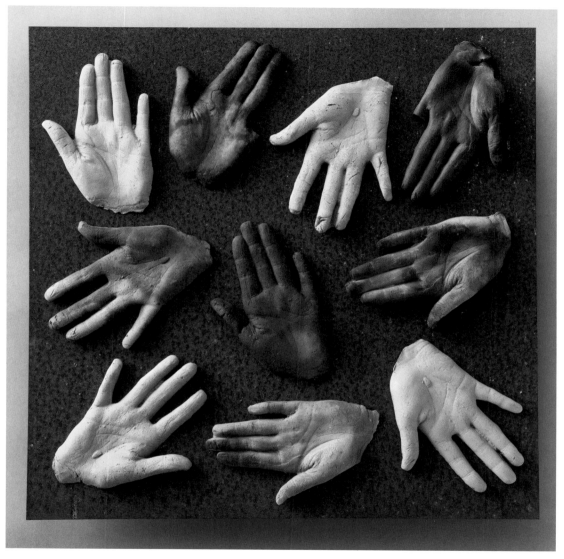

A signature wall piece featuring
clay hands.

experimenters have reaped the wellspring of satisfaction and list of rewards that Woo's work has garnered. Woo started her journey into clay in the 1950s. Decades later she is hailed as a respected educator, researcher, curator, glaze alchemist and Chinese folk pottery preservationist.

A 1998 grant from the Rockefeller Foundation paved the way for Woo and two co-curators, Susanne and John Stephenson, to spend over a decade scouring rural China in search of vanishing pottery traditions. The research culminated with the *International Chinese Folk Pottery Exhibition/Symposium & Films* in 2013 at the University of Michigan Museum of Art and a subsequent travelling exhibition, *Chinese Folk Pottery: The Art of the Everyday.*

Woo is the 12th metro Detroit artist to earn the coveted Eminent Artist Award from The Kresge Foundation. Since 2008, the award has celebrated the lifelong professional achievements of some of the region's most dedicated artists and the contributions that their creativity has added to the cultural landscape. Each year, the Kresge Arts in Detroit office, administered by the College for Creative Studies, convenes a panel of artists and arts professionals to make the selection. The award includes a $50,000 unrestricted prize.

"Marie Woo has been a transformational force in the development and elevation of her art form, and in the enrichment of our cultural community — the basis for the Kresge Eminent Artist Award," says Rip Rapson, the president and CEO of The Kresge Foundation. "On the one hand, she is a prominent student of deep

The lone portrait of Marie's relatives in Seattle, Washington, 1920.

traditions, including Chinese folk pottery, with all of its functional beauty. On the other hand, she is a dynamo within the contemporary practice of ceramics that challenges conventional notions of function and beauty. Her creations reflect a phenomenal level of craft and a fluidity of mind to which we can all aspire."

The evidence of Woo's ceramic achievement stretches around the globe. Her works are housed in many of the world's leading museums, from the Detroit Institute of Arts and the Mills College Museum of Art in Oakland, California, to the former Leningrad Mukhina Institute of Art in Russia and museums in Greece, China and Latvia, among others.

Woo is the first Kresge Eminent Artist honored for a lifetime of work in ceramics.

"Marie is just this singularly inspirational figure," says James Adair, who has known Woo since the 1970s and is president of the Michigan Ceramic Arts Association (MCAA). "She's very productive, but not in the sense of production for production's sake." In 2019, MCAA presented Woo with its lifetime artist achievement award. The honor followed *A Clay Odyssey*, a 50-work 2016 retrospective of Woo's career at the Birmingham Bloomfield Art Center in Michigan.

Through a spirit of playful, and sometimes accidental, investigation, Woo's body of work obliterates the line between form and function. "Her bowls are bowls," explains Adair, who is also a clay artist, "but it's not like you're ever going to put potatoes in them. They celebrate the bowl form, but in her hands they also become alive. Marie takes the craft and just transforms it to another level altogether."

Across her body of work, one sees the same traits. Woo creates a portal, through which she and viewers simultaneously question and re-imagine the limits of form, and the necessity of function. And it is through her unapologetic willingness to push clay in new directions that Woo's creations continuously stretch the medium into fine art, often with the aid of whatever surrounds her, including natural elements such as rain, snow, even the stray markings of twigs.

Ask Woo about her tendency toward play and she sums it up in her characteristically thoughtful yet direct way. "I just love clay. From the moment I touched it, I became addicted," she says. The idea that more is at work — perhaps creative excellence or ceramic innovation — Woo leaves to others. Collectors and art

A series of unfired pieces Marie
exposed to natural elements.

critics generally describe both as omnipresent in Woo's ceramic technique. "The clay guides," Marie says. "I can only yield and flow with its rhythms."

Embedded in those few words are clues to some of the mystery within Woo's enduring love of clay. In her hands, the transformation of each piece becomes a quiet connection with the philosophy that has shaped her life since the 1960s — Taoism, the Chinese belief system that promotes harmony and ease as a force present in all things. It is not Woo's way to declare mastery of such things. But to watch her is to see an embodiment of one of the Tao's most important principles, *Wu Wei* [*woo way*] — literally "effortless action" in Chinese, and sometimes translated simply as "flow."

Of course Woo insists that she is only what she's always been: a student, ever curious, ever exploring. "Clay is a challenge, really. It's from the earth. It's not intellectual; it's very intuitive, not rushed," she explains. "That's what stimulates me," she says. "It's like solving a problem. You go one step forward, two steps backwards, then, maybe, you trust."

Eventually the potter, who is in tune with the clay more than with any perceived outcome, learns, Woo says, to prize process over perfection. "Sometimes you put a piece in the kiln and you think it's going to come out the way you hoped, and it comes out totally different, a real surprise," Marie says. "You learn to be patient, not to be expecting too much."

Marie and Harvey in Nepal, 1965.

Let all things take their course.

LAO-TZU

I woke up in bits, like all children,
piecemeal over the years.

ANNIE DILLARD

Marie Woo was not raised to believe in breaking molds or creating new ones.

She was born April 3, 1928, in an era — and in a home — where tradition held that the biggest fortunes and brightest futures belonged to boys. Her parents, Chinese immigrants, lavished both their daughters with love, constancy and the comfort of familial routine. Nothing was spared except the vision that either daughter, Mabel or Marie, might rise above gender-based barriers, or one day be hailed internationally as an artistic trailblazer.

"When I was growing up, I'd do the things boys could do, like sports, and bicycling. My father used to say, 'You should've been a boy,'" she said. "My sister … she wanted to study medicine. He says, 'Oh, you're a girl.' So, she went to pharmacy school and studied to be a pharmacist."

Woo chooses to laugh rather than lament about this lone detail of an otherwise "pretty routine" childhood in Seattle's Chinatown neighborhood. "It's funny now, in those days," she says, "people just didn't think of women ever being in certain, maybe any, professions. It was just the way."

Woo's parents came to Seattle separately, immigrating from the southern part of China. Her father, Henry, arrived when he was 13. Her mother, Jushi, came later, around 1920.

As open as Woo's father was about his belief in the dominance of boys, he was noticeably vague about the details of his own profession. "A neighborhood businessman," is what Woo recalls. "I don't think it was legal," she says, erupting into laughter before continuing. "He ran a series of lottery houses."

Woo smiles when she thinks of her mother, a housewife with a sharp eye for detail and a penchant for creative expression as well. "Every winter, we'd have new sweaters. She loved to make things."

But it would be a grade school teacher who noticed and nurtured Woo's creativity. "My parents had no interest in art. It was never an important thing." Her parents did, however, prioritize strong education and sent Woo and her older sister Mabel to a Chinese study school each day following classes at their elementary school. As a young girl, Woo enjoyed expressing herself through drawing. "It came naturally. I just followed it."

Trust your natural responses;
and everything will fall into place.
LAO-TZU

I discovered myself and the world, and
then forgot them, and discovered them again.
ANNIE DILLARD

Looking back, it makes sense that Marie Woo's love affair with clay sprang to life in a serene elemental setting on the water.

"A friend in Seattle had a houseboat, and she had a wheel and kiln on it. That was the first time I touched clay," Woo says. The precise date has long since left her memory. But the impact of the moment lingers. "I loved everything about it. I had been studying just general arts. But when I touched the clay, there was a feeling, a real responsiveness to material."

It was the 1950s. Woo was a fresh-eyed art student with a new bachelor of fine arts degree from the University of Washington in Seattle. She'd also completed general arts studies at the California College of Arts. But it was undeniably that one moment with her hands immersed in clay that gave instant shape and direction to Woo's path as an artist.

Through various arts circles she heard of a teacher in Michigan, just outside Detroit, who was making magic with clay and teaching graduate students how to configure classical functional forms into unmistakable fine art. "I don't know where I first heard about her," Woo recalls, referring to Maija Grotell, a Finnish-American ceramicist who founded the studio-based ceramics program at the Cranbrook Academy of Art. "But I heard and I said, she's the person I want to study with. I came to Detroit because of her."

Grotell, known as the "Mother of American Ceramics," would go on to leave the first major imprint on Woo's life as an artist.

"I am always drawn to the vessel form. So, when I make pieces for the wall, they're also shallow vessel forms. But then conceptually they are quite different. They're nonfunctional. ... I like to do both, and I like to do them in a way that is not stiff."

A row of traditional wood-fired Asian dragon kilns, Guizhou, China, 2002.

"I was profoundly influenced by her," says Woo, who studied with Grotell for two years before graduating with a master's of fine arts degree from Cranbrook, which opened its doors in 1932 as a student-centric laboratory for contemporary art and design studies, and quickly began to shape the studio arts movement. "Maija believed that individuals have the creative capacity within and it is our responsibility to search deeply for the essence of making meaningful work."

Today, ceramic experts and observers point to very specific traces of Grotell's influence in Woo's artistry. "You can tell instantly that Marie studied with Maija," said MaryAnn Wilkinson, executive director of the Scarab Club and one of six panelists who selected Woo as the 2020 Kresge Eminent Artist.

One obvious place to note Grotell's influence is in the adherence to traditional shape that many of her vessels start with despite inevitably challenging all notions of function. Evidence also exists in the careful and considered attention that Woo poured into formulating glazes, cooking up precise recipes for the glass coating that gives gleam to the surfaces of pottery pieces. "Artist as alchemist" is how some describe Woo's careful technique. Other ceramicists strive to recreate and use "Woo Yellow," "Woo Blue," and "Woo Brown" — three of the best-known signature glazes that she created during her career.

If there's any truth to the talk of her mastery, the ever-humble Woo says it is owed in equal measure to Grotell. "She excelled in her glazes, and she inspired this confidence in you to find your voice. She was really just fabulous to learn from."

In 1956, Woo, the newly minted Cranbrook grad, began the first of a string of jobs teaching ceramics, and working as an apprentice in various parts of the U.S. and Asia. Stop No. 1: The University of Michigan, Ann Arbor. There, Woo wasted no time returning what she'd learned. "I loved working with the students in the studio, helping them learn the technique and the possibilities of the materials."

Like Grotell, Woo's passion as a teacher was obvious and infectious. "I consider myself so lucky that Marie was my first true ceramics teacher," says ceramicist Roberta Griffith, one of Woo's earliest and most well-known students.

"She was a first-year teacher when I met her. But she was so hands-on and giving in the studio and with her love of preparing the kiln. She didn't withhold anything from her students. All of her secrets and her recipes she shared freely."

Prior to stumbling upon Woo's class, Griffith, now 82, had been set to pursue painting and drawing. "I don't think she has a clue just how much she inspired my love of ceramics. It changed the course of my life.

"When I became a teacher and whenever I traveled to teach or study with other ceramicists around the world, I made a point to share everything I learned as well. It's one of Marie's great influences and that spirit is why she's so respected," Griffith says.

One of the highlights of Griffith's career, she says, was having a chance some years ago to give back to Marie. "I have had a lifelong affinity for copper red glazes," she explains. "I was so thrilled when Marie asked me to give her one of my best copper red plates for a collection that she was developing at UM. She's usually the one giving inspiration and so much of herself to others."

She who is centered in the Tao

can go wherever she wishes without danger.

LAO-TZU

You can't test courage

cautiously.

ANNIE DILLARD

The best teachers are said never to cease being students. At UM, the maxim proved true again and again for Woo.

First, she met James Plumer, a professor of Far Eastern Art History. Plumer was a renowned expert on temmoku pottery, a style dating back to China's Song Dynasty (960–1279 AD). In his travels, he uncovered historic kiln sites from that era. "He was this storehouse of knowledge about Chinese art and culture, and ceramics was his love," Marie recalls.

Over tea, Plumer would captivate Woo with stories and photo slides, and an insistence that she select her cup carefully. "I'd go to pick up a teacup, and he would say, 'Oh no, pick a Song Dynasty one.'"

Plumer died in 1972, but Marie still cherishes his influence. "He was the one who got me interested in Asian ceramics. I knew nothing," she said. Plumer also opened Woo's eyes to culture too, namely Taoism, the belief system credited to philosopher Lao-Tzu. "He inspired exciting and vast horizons previously unknown to me."

Those seeds of curiosity began to flourish when Woo, who was still new and enthusiastic to teaching, welcomed Japanese potter Kaneshige Toyo into her classroom. His visit instantly altered everything Woo thought she knew about pottery's possibilities as a form of expression. "I was absolutely amazed by him," Marie recalls.

Toyo had been invited to UM shortly after being designated as Japan's first

Marie and Harvey in
Japan, 1965.

"living national cultural treasure," in salute to his research and rediscovery of 16th century clay and kiln preparation techniques developed during Japan's Momoyama art period.

Watching Toyo display some of the techniques gave Woo her first encounter with the importance of ceramic preservation. "Where he came from, he did not use glazes. My students and I, we'd never seen ceramic done like that."

Toyo, she said, "let the clay do the work. It was not an absolute control but one of ease and harmony. The beauty was so natural," Woo said. "We were making tight little Swedish pots with small openings, but without the softness and sensitivity of form."

At the end of Toyo's visit, he extended an open invitation for Woo to study with him at a small pottery village in Bizen, Japan. While faculty colleagues chided her for even considering abandoning the stability of job at a prestigious institution, Woo's intuition screamed: *Go*. And she did without regret.

For three years Woo turned Bizen, with its coastline views and history as home to Japan's oldest and most revered pottery style, into a private classroom. She steeped herself in the mysteries of unfired clay. Some of the techniques dated as far back as the sixth century. Woo immersed herself completely, determined to absorb all that she could about the skills required to master Bizen pottery's signature raw textures and tones, and the quiet culture at its root.

"When I learned the Asian technique, it was a whole new revelation for me," she said. "I experienced an environment of tranquility and ease of expression that I'd never known. My time spent there changed everything. I'm sure it was meant to happen."

Japan altered Woo's life in another major way. There she married the love of her life, Harvey Levine. They married at the American Embassy in Tokyo in 1959, where Levine eventually landed work as a young architect. Woo had met Levine while they each studied at Cranbrook. When she chose Japan, he boarded a plane, too. First stop: Long Beach, California. From there they decided to take the long way via a slow cargo ship. Woo has since forgotten how

A moment of rest for Marie's hands.

long they traveled. But the feeling and the importance of the choice are etched. "It was the start of an exciting time for both of us. A real adventure."

From Japan, the couple spent much of the 1960s winding through Southeast Asia — with visits to Vietnam, Cambodia, Thailand, Kathmandu, and less developed parts of India. True to the creative spirit of the times, they travelled mostly via a Volkswagen bus they purchased in Singapore and later sold to a prince in India. "We were very young," she said. "We thought we'd just keep going."

Then life intervened.

"If I hadn't come at the moment that I did, I'm sure they would have continued traveling throughout Asia indefinitely," says son Ian Levine, a 54-year-old corporate pilot. "Mom still talks about what a special time it was."

Levine was born in Bangkok, where Woo taught ceramics at Chulalongkorn University. Her passion for art and the freedom of travel remained strong, but Woo also began to feel a tug toward "normalcy." "People we'd met on the road travelling started to write us saying, we have a front porch, a driveway, a washer and dryer," she said. "We started to think maybe we should go home, too."

"After continuous striving there comes a time when the conscious mind yields control and ideas will evolve slowly and naturally."

The Master never reaches for the great;
thus she achieves greatness.

LAO-TZU

Hone and spread your spirit till
you yourself are a sail.

ANNIE DILLARD

The family's return to America in 1967 included its share of winding roads. There were brief stops in Seattle and Minneapolis. Then off to suburban Detroit, which offered the greatest promise of opportunity for Levine's career as an architect, and Woo's multiple roles of mother, studio-based potter, and sought-after teacher.

Eighteen months later, the couple welcomed a playmate for Ian, a daughter named Leslie, and Levine eventually designed the family's home in West Bloomfield Township, just a few miles from the Cranbrook campus where he and Marie met. The house, on a secluded lane and surrounded by nature, came complete with a basement studio and ample space for Woo to create her own kilns, to begin infusing her vessels with the gifts of her travels: a sense of flow, an openness to experimentation, and the guidance of a new teacher, her own intuition.

In retrospect, Woo says, making art while mothering was perhaps the most challenging period of her life. "I don't know how I managed it all," she said with a chuckle. "There were days when I would rush from teaching directly to a freezing hockey practice, or leave an orchestra rehearsal to anxiously check cones in my kiln. I'm honestly amazed. But I think they turned out pretty OK."

To Ian, her son, Woo moved seamlessly between her roles. "If my mother wasn't busy trying to create something, it was, what do you want to make today? To this day, you could take either of us to pretty much any clay studio and we'd

Marie prepares a piece for one of the outdoor kilns she built at her home in West Bloomfield Township, Michigan.

know what to do because of her. She made her worlds become one, which was really a gift to my sister and me."

Wilkinson, of the Scarab Club, says Woo has been just as much of a gift to the Detroit area arts community. "Though not originally from the area, she chose to spend her long, productive career in metro Detroit."

Woo also chose to extend her interest beyond the studio. She dedicated a full decade to documenting and preserving the vanishing art of Chinese folk pottery. Through her various trips to China, she amassed more than 100 pieces collected from remote villages where the tradition of making unfired functional vessels had flourished. Everything that Woo learned through her research she brought back to Michigan, determined to share with scholars and potters across the state. About 40 pieces of the collection were featured in a nationally travelling exhibit.

For Woo, the real beauty of her project continues to be that it emerged more by accident than grand design. One day in 1995, while in China for a Tai Chi conference, Woo was practicing the meditative martial art outdoors when she caught her first glimpse of Minyao. She was struck by the rawness of the pottery style made in kilns throughout rural China and designed for everyday use. At the time, Woo was more familiar with Guanyao, the famously delicate style of pottery made for royal use and export around the world.

She saw pieces being sold on the streets but soon learned that back in the villages, the folk tradition was vanishing. "In the West we knew nothing about this kind of folk stuff," says Woo. With Ian and Leslie heading off to college, Woo had time for a full immersion. "I thought it might be interesting. I wrote for a grant, and I got it. So I had to go."

Between annual trips to China, two other passion projects closer to home continued to call to her as well.

The educator in her couldn't resist a chance to help fight for the preservation of classes at Pewabic Pottery, a National Historic Landmark ceramic tile studio founded in Detroit in 1903 by Mary Chase Stratton, a kindred ceramicist with a shared passion for arts education advocacy. As part of her lobbying, Woo joined Pewabic's board of trustees, taught classes, and became a vocal champion for more than a decade advocating for classes to be held sacred even in the midst of plummeting revenue. "Back then, they were always in the red. But a friend and I believed, you don't make it better by cutting education. Now there's a waiting list."

Woo, the artist, kept busy too, her full-time focus — finally— on fire. "It was a selfishly good feeling to have almost all the hours of the day to myself again."

On a whim, she became a pivotal member of the Clay Ten, an experimental traveling ceramics collective formed in 1983. The group spent roughly a decade conceiving and creating ways to showcase the works of the 10 potters who had been struggling to find welcoming outlets for their art.

"Artists tend to work in isolation which was true for Clay Ten folks too," recalls Woo. Becoming a founding member "made me listen to another artist, and realize how much the exchange of ideas with an open mind can create inspiring and stimulating energy, new aesthetic concepts, harmony, and mutual respect."

After years of watching Woo fuse her interests, son Ian has come to believe

Woo shows off a porcelain wall piece on display in her home. Like many of her works, the piece is unnamed.

her most creative gift may not emanate from clay at all. "Her attention to detail is something that's true across everything she does," he says. "She looks, and once she decides, she dives in and just naturally finds the essence of whatever she's doing."

Oddly enough, it is ease that now challenges Woo the most as she stands at the twilight of her career. To family, friends and fans alike, she has said that she is on her way into retirement. Her studio is dark, empty of all evidence of the art she unleashed there, save for a single potter's wheel. "I'm really trying to retire, but the ideas and opportunities keep coming." Sometimes she visits a fellow ceramicist in nearby Keego Harbor who allows use of his kiln. "It's not easy to exit."

In 2019, she seemed closer than ever to closure. Then the phone rang with an invitation for a fall 2020 solo exhibition at Detroit's Scarab Club Art Gallery. The phone rang once more with a call from Kresge Arts in Detroit, and news that she had been selected as the 2020 Kresge Eminent Artist. The surprise announcement left her suspicious and flabbergasted. "I'm in my 90s," she said. "I have to think; what am I going to do with $50,000? It's overwhelming."

Coming to terms with the fullness of the Kresge honor and its timing also brings Woo face-to-face with the philosophical aspects of clay, the subtle ways the relationship has kept her engaged yet at ease with life, year after year, after year. "Clay is really a journey all these years. It's amazing. The years, they went so quickly."

In many ways, Woo's work at the wheel and in the world has been akin, she says, to that of the poet. "It's the economy of language, the essence of a thing. Poets work a lifetime to do it. I think artists and potters are the same. None of us can go on forever."

**Her name will be held in honor
from generation to generation.**
LAO-TZU

Nichole Christian is a writer and veteran journalist. She is co-author of *Canvas Detroit*. Her writing also appears in *Portraits 9/11/01: The Collected Portraits of Grief* from *The New York Times*; the online arts journal, *Essay'd, A Detroit Anthology*; and *Dear Dad: Reflections on Fatherhood*. She was creative director, editor and lead writer of *A Life Speaks,* the monograph honoring 2019 Kresge Eminent Artist Gloria House.

This essay features select excerpts from: *Tao Te Ching: A New English Version* by Stephen Mitchell, and *The Abundance* by Annie Dillard.

"I never thought of it, but if my work can inspire people that's great. I just do what I do."

Select voices on
Marie Woo's
ceramic journey

MARKS ON MANY

SPARK FROM AFAR

Inside Woo's wondrous influence on other women makers

Mary Barringer

How does an artist become?

The world is greatly enriched by all those who channel their creativity into gardens, parenting, cooking, and a thousand other unsung endeavors. But few people take the inexplicable step of calling themselves artists and what they create art.

To declare oneself an artist is a stubborn, prideful, maybe foolish act of self-assertion and faith. How would a young person form such an idea about herself? Talent may have helped early on to float her apart from her peers, but talent alone would not sustain her for the long journey. Encouragement, temperament and luck will certainly matter, but a crucial spark often comes from the example of an older artist who, by the simple fact of who she is, embodies the possibility.

Marie Woo and I belong to different generations, live in different parts of the country, and did not meet until I was in my 40s. We appeared to have but two things in common: we are women and we work in clay. Although I was 20 years along my own artistic road before we met, I had known of her for a long time. As a young artist in New England I had heard her name and seen her work, distinctive for its touch, its ambition, and its bold but sensitive interpretation of Asian clay traditions. From afar I had formed an idea of her as a fellow traveler in this clay world we shared.

In those days — the early 1970s — the names of only a few women stood out in the clay landscape. Woo herself had been lucky to have studied with one

An example of Marie's signature glaze work and her deep knowledge of foundational forms.

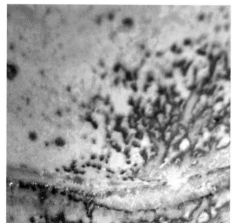

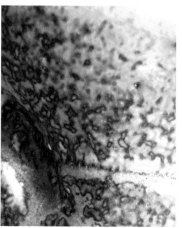

Ceramicist Maija Grotell overlooks her students at the Cranbrook Academy of Art in 1939.

of the great figures of mid-century ceramics, Maija Grotell, and thereby to see at close range the life of a woman artist. I have no doubt that she in turn served as an exemplar to many of her female students, but her influence spread far beyond that immediate circle. Once planted in the soil of her own studio practice, her work and the artist behind it sent out tendrils of influence in unknown directions, nourishing the dreams of many a young maker crafting her own artist-self. I count myself fortunate to have been one of them.

Mary Barringer has worked in clay since 1973, making both sculpture and functional pottery. She has exhibited her work internationally and taught at universities and craft centers across the U.S. In addition to her studio work she has written and lectured on the history of ceramics, and from 2004–2014 was the editor of the *Studio Potter* journal. She lives in western Massachusetts.

SPARK FROM AFAR

"The ideas are induced by the Chi, the great and involuntary rhythm of life that can work the subconscious, the body, the limbs, the fingers, and into the clay."

"When you think of vessel form, you think of function but not necessarily so when I make vessels. I make bowls, which people call them tea bowls, but I call them maybe for cornflakes. They can be."

The maker and mother as one

Leslie Raymond

My mom, Marie, fondly refers to the period in her life before my brother Ian and I were born as "Marie B.C." Yet the relationship between Marie's work as an artist, *before children*, and her life as a mother was always fluid.

Some of my clearest childhood memories involve painting and making things out of clay under my mom's watchful eye. She enjoyed sharing that creative space with me. She would gently guide my process, laying a groundwork that would inform my art practice to this day.

After a magnificent chapter of her life with my dad working and traveling overseas, my parents returned to southeast Michigan where they had first met as graduate students at Cranbrook. In 1980, we moved into an incredible house in West Bloomfield Township that my architect dad designed. My mom slab-rolled and salt-glazed tiles for the kitchen and mudroom. She invited me to decorate a couple of them, which were laid in with the rest when they were installed. Her family and creative lives were fused.

Her studio was in the lower level. One side was made up entirely of sliding glass doors with a view of "the jungle," as they called their barely-tamed two-acre wooded lot. The woods sloped down a hill, and at the bottom was her open-air kiln shed. Over the years, she modified and reworked her assortment of kilns.

Marie's philosophy on kiln building reflects her approach to so many things. In constant collaboration with the materials at hand, she magically combines them to create new, perfectly realized things that seem to come into being on

A young Leslie Raymond playing in one of her mother's large pots, circa 1973.

their own. "When I want to build a kiln, I ask your dad for help and he starts drawing," she told me. "Six weeks later, he's still drawing! Me, I just look around at the bricks I have and start stacking them up. When they're all used up, the kiln is done." Marie always chose to fire at night so that the neighbors wouldn't see the smoke and worry that someone's house was burning down.

I feel fortunate that my mom stayed at home and raised us, and welcomed us into the inspired and absorbing world of her studio. As kids, we were not allowed to have Play-Doh. I felt deprived but I also knew how lucky I was to get to play with the real stuff. We dined on her "rejects," and if something ever broke, she would never be the slightest bit upset. "Don't worry about it!" she would say.

My mom worked in her studio every day — even if only for a short while, always slow and steady, and at times prolific. She always found time for teaching too, including at what was then known as the Birmingham Art Association, for blue-haired ladies who golfed on Wednesday and did pottery class on Thursday. From this I learned how deeply hands-on crafts experience could fortify lifelong art appreciation. As a child, my mom was just my mom. I didn't comprehend that she was an artist with an intensely committed and disciplined practice, and I am so grateful to have witnessed that.

Marie with her daughter, Leslie, and granddaughter Lalena Stevens during her 2018 career retrospective, *A Clay Odyssey*, at the Birmingham Bloomfield Art Center.

Marie displays the tattoo that she and Leslie chose in celebration of Mother's Day in 2000.

Though she never talked to me about paving the way for other people, I am now able to see how her discipline and dedication have inspired others in the field, particularly women, who are as determined as she is to create no matter what.

At 92, even as she tries to finally retire, she remains devoted and intent on sharing. Not long ago, my daughter Lalena had a chance to work with Marie on the wheel. Determined to pass on her love of clay, even as she was beginning a huge deaccession process, my mom sent a bag of clay and clay tools over for her granddaughter. Lalena keeps the bag in her playroom, also known as "Studio LS."

At my daughter's urging, we recently took it out. Together, we've begun to slowly, like my mom, "make some stuff."

Leslie Raymond is Marie Woo's second-born child and only daughter. She is also Executive Director of the Ann Arbor Film Festival. As a longtime teaching media artist, Raymond founded the New Media Program at the University of Texas at San Antonio, where she worked as an assistant professor of art.

MARIE UNDIVIDED

"I love working with rusty metal. You leave the metal outside and it just changes. Nature helps without me doing anything."

A mission to make clay matter

Tom Phardel

When I received the news that Marie Woo had received The Kresge Foundation's 2020 Eminent Artist Award, I felt that the chaos of our present world had been made right again.

I have been fortunate to have known and worked with Marie Woo for over 45 years now as a fellow artist, educator and Detroit arts advocate. In each of these areas Marie has imparted great wisdom, generosity of spirit and a quite steady determination within the greater clay community. In my mind there are two words that define Marie Woo's work as an artist: fresh and direct.

In the early years of our friendship, which began in the '70s, she expressed her ideas through "the vessel format." Her works seemed to be influenced by the Japanese philosophy *Wabi Sabi*, beauty found in the imperfect nature of life.

Marie poked, tore or scratched the surfaces. Once the material was thrown on the wheel, she would re-construct the vessel form with total confidence, never overworked. The forms were sparse, and the marked surfaces read like paintings.

Marie has fought to push ceramics forward not just through her works but also as a committed advocate for the arts and for her love of clay.

During the 1980s and '90s ceramics had a hard time getting any exposure. So Marie became one of the founding members of Clay Ten, a group of 10 metro Detroit ceramic artists. In those years, ceramic works were generally looked at as hobby or as just straight craft, never fine art. As the Clay Ten, we believed we were much stronger than one artist out to open minds and that together we

Marie and Tom Phardel in conversation at Pewabic Pottery.

could expand our medium. Making our own decisions, working structure and community proved very beneficial to all the members. Marie was one of the strongest pillars throughout.

We actively exhibited and fought for the ceramic medium to be considered equal to the other fine art mediums of painting and sculpture. We organized our own exhibitions, finding venues sometimes in vacant spaces throughout Detroit. Notably, Clay Ten staged an exhibition at the Willis Gallery, in Detroit, in the mid-'80s. Marie's technique was direct and to the point, almost primal. These works paid homage to the vessel tradition, yet clearly pushed the boundaries towards an abstract expressionism and gesture.

Since the late 1990s, Marie started creating pure sculptural works. Again, sparse and primal in their construction, they addressed form relationships. Fast-forward 35 years from Clay Ten's early days, to 2019: at 91 she shocked every-one at the Buckham Gallery's "Big Clay" exhibition in Flint, Michigan. Marie

L–R. John Glick, Marie, and Tom Phardel at the Birmingham Bloomfield Art Center during the opening of Marie's *Clay Odyssey* exhibit in 2018.

exhibited a magnificent saturated indigo blue wall installation that floated freely in space. This piece clearly demonstrated to me that Marie is still freely experimenting and searching, continuing to investigate new frontiers.

In a time of endless self-promotion via social media, Marie represents something quite different, quietly behind the scenes leaving her mark through her work, steadfastness and generosity to the arts community. We are all the beneficiaries of a lifetime of effort.

Well done, Marie!

Tom Phardel is a sculptor, ceramicist, curator and longtime arts educator. His work is included in the permanent collection of The Detroit Institute of Arts. Phardel, a founding member of Clay Ten, is the retired chair of the Ceramics Department at Detroit's College for Creative Studies, a position he held for 35 years.

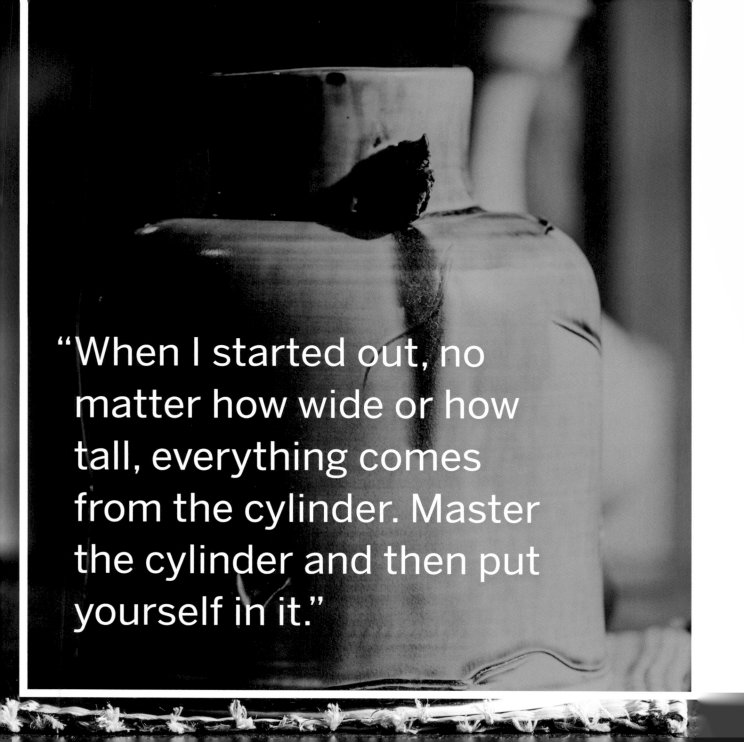

"When I started out, no matter how wide or how tall, everything comes from the cylinder. Master the cylinder and then put yourself in it."

Woo's roots as an educator revisited

Steve McBride

Marie Woo has had a major impact on the field of ceramics: inventing new glazes, altering forms, challenging notions of function and beauty. She has blurred the boundaries of fine art and pottery.

Watching Marie in the studio is a joy. Moving with a casual, Zen-like ease, she approaches the clay with an open, curious mind and an infectious "Let's go with it" sense of adventure. She seems relaxed, centered ... but there's always a twinkle in her eye that hints at the creative journey to come.

That spirit creates a sense of freedom and looseness in Marie's art. She never overthinks things. Her approach towards clay is always straightforward and direct: "Let's try this; maybe it will work, maybe it won't." That attitude is refreshing and liberating to a student, imbuing the entire studio with a sense of possibility. Art for Marie is an adventure. And her energy is inspiring.

For me, though, Marie's impact is more personal. Her inspiring energy helped to shape the character of Pewabic Pottery, Detroit's National Historic Landmark pottery founded in 1903.

Marie was a key player in 1981 when Pewabic became an independent nonprofit organization. As a teacher and board member, she helped Detroit's historic pottery find new life. She was an early and fierce champion of Pewabic's education program, even when the economics of it didn't make sense. Marie recognized education as a crucial part of who we were, dating back to the pottery's earliest days.

ABOVE AND LEFT Marie attending a
Raku firing event at Pewabic Pottery
in the 1990s.

Pewabic has always had a legacy of strong, visionary women. I'm sure Marie
would have found a kindred spirit in our founder, Mary Chase Perry Stratton.
Like Marie, Mary Stratton was both artist and teacher — helping shape the
visual fabric of Detroit and crafting inspiring tile installations across the U.S.,
but equally influential in helping launch the ceramics programs at the University
of Michigan, Wayne State University, and the Society for Arts & Crafts (which
would become the College for Creative Studies in Detroit).

It makes sense that Marie Woo would find a second home in Pewabic. The
studio and school were the foundation for ceramic art in Michigan. As a champion of folk craft, Marie must have been inspired by the history and the opportunity to sustain a tradition. As a teaching artist, she knew that education was
a way to keep that history vital and alive. That is a role she continues to play,
inspiring our students today.

Her love of clay remains at the heart of all that she does. Centering clay
is one of the first skills a potter learns. It's an essential step before beginning

A playful Marie giving shape to a new form. Residency in Fuping, China, 2007

to shape the pot, but the task of coaxing a lump of clay into symmetry at the center of a potter's wheel is an art of its own. For a beginner, it usually comes as an "Aha!" moment when the clay suddenly starts spinning smoothly between your palms. Everything feels balanced, in harmony. You are at one with the clay. This is a moment of infinite creative possibilities, when the clay can take many shapes.

When I think about Marie, I think of that moment, and the way her works remind us of its power. It's what makes her a living national treasure.

As I write this in March 2020, the nation is just beginning to realize the terrifying scope of a world health crisis not seen in a century. Now, more than ever, the world needs art to comfort and inspire us. Even more, we need the spirit that Marie Woo brings to the world — calm, peaceful, accepting uncertainty and radiating joy.

Steve McBride is executive director of Pewabic Pottery. He is also a ceramic artist.

"I strive to be intuitive
and spontaneous
in my work."

"In '95, I went to a Tai Chi conference in China. I noticed that folk pottery, folk art was becoming rarer and more rarer ... and people weren't paying attention, because China was modernizing so fast."

PERSISTENT PRESERVATIONIST

A journey beyond the wheel

Margaret Carney

When Marie Woo contacted me in 1997, there was no Google search tool available. I only learned a bit about her from my colleague at the New York State College of Ceramics at Alfred University, ceramic artist Val Cushing. Marie wanted to study my dissertation. I was honored.

My 1980s doctoral research focused on the Song dynasty Cizhou wares recovered archaeologically from Julu, a marketplace in southern Hebei Province, inundated by a flood of the Yellow River in 1108. These jars, bowls, pillows and ewers that were everyday people's wares were discovered in 1918 when farmers digging wells during a drought uncovered these 800-year-old Song dynasty buried treasures.

I shipped the 400-pages-plus publication to her and in return the next month I not only got back my loaned book, but additionally I received a beautiful Marie Woo bowl that I treasure. I managed to locate our correspondence from 1997, revealing that she had included her China trip itinerary in the box and had invited me to meet her and her colleagues on the second half of their travels. She had found the bibliography of my dissertation "helpful." Unfortunately, for years I remained in the dark about the discoveries made during that China excursion.

After my husband and I moved to Ann Arbor in the summer of 2012, I began to discover that Marie Woo was more than a well-known potter and beloved educator. That September I was invited to moderate a panel discussion at the *International Chinese Folk Pottery Symposium* in conjunction with the exhibition and film viewings in January 2013 at the University of Michigan Museum of Art. The local organizers included Marie Woo, Susanne Stephenson, Georgette Zirbes, Susan Crowell and Natsu Oyobe.

The story of Marie's deep connection with Chinese folk pottery began more than a decade earlier. She was concerned that the traditional Chinese folk pottery, or *Minyao,* was being lost during the modernization of China. These weren't imperial wares made at government run kilns, but rather the everyday pottery made locally and used by ordinary Chinese people. The potters, kilns and pottery sites devoted to folk pottery for hundreds if not thousands of years were located over the vast country that is China. She believed that documenting these diverse Chinese folk pottery traditions would at least provide a written and visual record of the traditions that might otherwise be lost. She received a grant from the Asian Cultural Council in 1998 to begin research on Chinese folk pottery. This provided support for her to travel, research and document pottery and kilns in remote traditional villages throughout China.

Her fellow travelers, researchers, documenters and pottery collectors in China varied through the next decade or so but included John Stephenson, Susanne Stephenson, Jackson Li and Georgette Zirbes. Marie was on every trip to the more than 20 sites where folk pottery was collected, potters were interviewed, historical information was recorded and photo documentation was gathered. Ultimately, hundreds of examples of folk pottery from diverse Chinese peoples were collected.

To my knowledge, no one else thought to do this while these folk traditions lingered. And who would be better qualified to research and gather information about Chinese folk pottery, potters, and kilns than a potter, educator, collector, and knowledge-seeker?

I do not think it is inaccurate to describe Marie Woo as more than a preservationist. Like all inspirational women I've known, she has a vision, is motivated, recognizes opportunities and seizes them. She sees things other people don't see. Her creativity and curiosity play well in these scenarios. She's a

Chinese pickle pot factory. The clay pieces are made in kilns across rural China.

LEFT A potter in Gui Zhou, China, brings pots in from the rain during one of Marie's trips to rural pottery villages throughout China.

BELOW Pieces of Chinese, Japanese, Mexican, Vietnamese, and Pueblo pottery that Marie has designated as gifts to universities.

person who gets shit done. She has an idea, sets a goal, and she figures out how to accomplish her goal.

For instance, it was her persistence that saw that a selection of the Chinese folk pottery and photographs from the exhibition that was on view at the University of Michigan Museum of Art in 2013 traveled nationally from 2013 to 2019. She arranged venues and speakers, and then donated pieces from the collection to the Smithsonian Institution's Freer Sackler Gallery, the Alfred Ceramics Museum, Michigan State University, as well as the University of Michigan Museum of Art.

When I shared on social media about her winning this prestigious Kresge award, there were literally hundreds of positive responses and comments from other ceramicists, collectors, former students, and colleagues locally and internationally, joyful responses from individuals who had taught alongside her, used her "Woo yellow" glaze, and enjoyed her "No B.S." attitude. She's an inspirational figure whether viewed as a potter, innovator, pioneer, explorer or leader. One artist shared an image of a watercolor she had created of a tea bowl titled "Watercolor, 2016, tea bowl, Woo Yellow." I think you can imagine how beautiful it is. One Facebook friend referred to her as a "National Treasure." Several Facebook responders simply said, "Thank you, Marie."

Margaret Carney is a ceramic historian who holds a PhD and master's degrees in Asian art history, and a BA in anthropology and archaeology. She is the founding director and curator of the International Museum of Dinnerware Design in Ann Arbor, Michigan.

Selected works

IN HARMONY

Vase

ca 1958
Stoneware, glazed
5¾ × 5 × 4¼
Alfred Ceramic Art Museum
Gift of William E. Pitney, William Pitney Collection
ACAM 1995.438
Purchased at the Detroit Artists Market

Footed bowl

ca 1958
Stoneware, glazed
3⅞ dia × 4⅜ h
Alfred Ceramic Art Museum
Gift of William E. Pitney, William Pitney Collection
ACAM 1995.406
Purchased at the Detroit Artists Market

Cylindrical vase

1965
Earthenware, glazed
6½ dia × 10 h
Mills College Art Museum
Gift of the Artist, Antonio Prieto Memorial Collection

Bowls

ca 1981
Porcelain, glazed
CLOCKWISE FROM TOP LEFT:
18 dia × 5 h
17 dia × 9 h
14 dia × 2 h
18 dia × 5 h

From the Detroit Institute of Arts
Michigan Artists 80/81 Exhibition
July 20–August 29, 1982

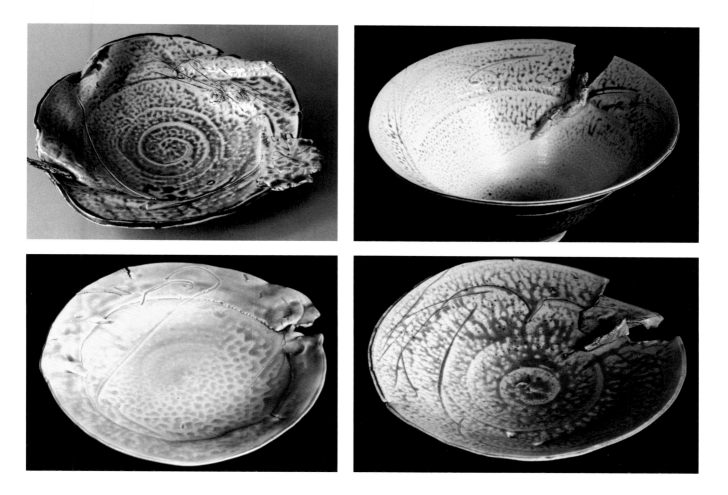

Untitled

1989
Porcelain with soda ash & straw glaze
19½ dia × 6⅝ h
Detroit Institute of Arts
Gift of Mrs. A. David Jones, Mrs. George Crane, Kathy
    Dambach, Mr. and Mrs. Tim Mast, and the Detroit
    Artists Market, 1989.93

Bowl

1991
Porcelain, soda-fired
20⅛ dia × 6½ h
Alfred Ceramic Art Museum
Museum purchase, Roger D. Corsaw Collection
ACAM 1992.55
Purchased from the Habatat/Shaw Gallery,
    Farmington, Michigan

Untitled

ca 1992
Porcelain, glazed
18½ × 18 × 3½
Collection of Tim & Marilyn Mast

Untitled

ca 2000
Stoneware, glazed
15 × 17 × 2
Collection of Tim & Marilyn Mast

Jar

2006
Porcelain with Woo ash glaze
8 dia × 9 h
Collection of the artist

Bowl

2006
Porcelain with Woo ash glaze
21 dia × 8 h
University of Michigan Museum of Art
Gift of the artist

Untitled

2010
Stoneware, glazed, with metal
9 × 8 × 7
Collection of the artist

Wall piece 6

2014
Porcelain, glazed
9½ × 12½ × 4
Collection of the artist

Wall piece 3

2014
Stoneware, glazed
13 × 5 × 2½
Collection of the artist

Untitled

2014
Stoneware, glazed
12 dia × 14 h
Collection of the artist

Wall piece 2

2016
Stoneware, glazed
15 × 17 × 2
Collection of the artist

Wall piece 4

2016
Clay mounted on kiln shelf
15 × 15 × 1¾
Collection of the artist

Wall piece 5

2016
Clay mounted on kiln shelf
21 × 21 × 1½
Collection of the artist

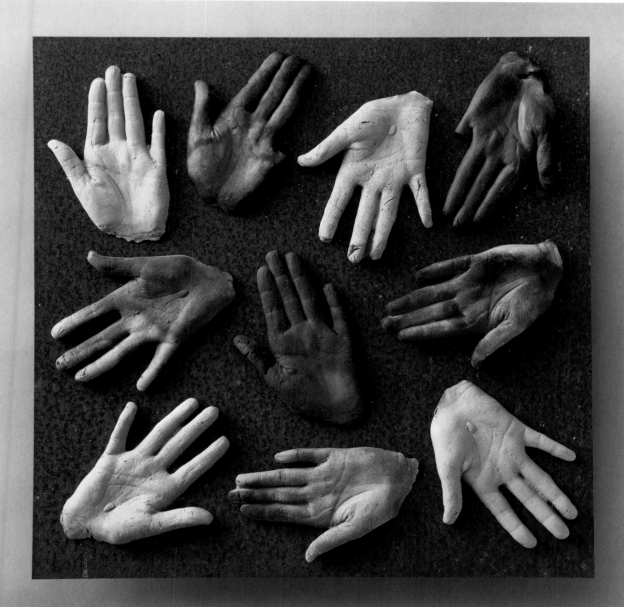

Untitled

2016
Porcelain, glazed
3½ × 7 × 8
Collection of Susanne Stephenson

Marie Woo

THE SPIRIT OF CHINESE POTTERY

I was introduced to the world of Asian art by Professor James Plumer, who was an art historian and colleague at the University of Michigan when I was teaching there. In 1935 he had made the important discovery of the Song Dynasty (A.D. 960–1280) temmoku kiln site in Fujian, China. I am grateful to my friend and mentor who served me tea in old celadon bowls while patiently lecturing about the Asian ceramics unknown but fascinating to me. Many years afterward I made the pilgrimage to the same ancient kiln site, where temmoku shards and pots still stuck in saggers were scattered all over the hillside, although the dragon kilns were long gone. Fingering the silent shards was an experience of listening to the past. It generated an involuntary link to the Song potter who made that work on a potter's wheel.

This beginning led me to investigate many other old and contemporary pottery kilns. I became aware of the Chinese pottery villages struggling to survive because there is now little demand for traditional pottery. The potters' lives have been transformed by their migration to the cities in search of a livelihood. Spurred by the global economy, China is dashing headlong into modernization and industrialization, leaving behind its rich cultural heritage in arts and crafts and architecture. In urban centers, whole old neighborhoods of traditional courtyard houses have been demolished and replaced by high-rise structures, and ancient city walls with their magnificent gates have been destroyed to make way for highways.

One of the many folk pottery villages and
kiln sites Marie visited during research trips
to China.

Toy whistles for festivals, Guizhou.

Roof tile typical of folk pottery style.

Peoples' lives have been disrupted, and the rich character of beautiful old cities such as Beijing has been obliterated. Until recently, remote rural villages were protected by distance from these fast-paced changes.

Unlike the sophisticated porcelains and fine imperial court ceramics, which are admired and collected by museums and widely documented, Chinese peasant pottery is relatively unrecognized. The Asian Cultural Council, a Rockefeller affiliate, provided the initial support for my travels to investigate and document folk pottery in China, a quest that became a complex journey into the unknown. China is geographically vast and diverse. The challenge has been daunting and often overwhelming, but the experience has been compelling, inspiring and always stimulating. I have traveled 10 years and many miles across China documenting contemporary folk pottery. I usually traveled with Li Jiansheng, an artist friend who is resourceful and knowledgeable about "all things Chinese."

He helped me plan itineraries and arranged for a small bus to fit a group of Michigan potters who were enthusiastic supporters of the project. Sometimes it was a challenge to reach remote destinations, and there were times we had to hike the last mile up steep narrow paths because our driver refused to take the

Teapot with dragon, peacock, and lotus figures, Jiangxi.

Ewer with copper green glaze, Hunan.

Fish on plates, bowls, and roof tiles (among other things) reflect the popularity of the fish as a symbol of prosperity.

A potter in Yunan, China, prepares a piece that will be fired in the style of everyday folk pottery, 2002.

bus any farther. Once we were rescued by a bulldozer that pulled our vehicle out of the deep red mud that covered the wheels.

Peoples' folk art is the essence of Chinese expression. In pottery, the long journey from the bold Neolithic Yangshou painted pots to the present-day utilitarian village pots is an awesome historical achievement. I have great admiration for the diversity and richness of creativity that so fascinates me. The amazing celadons, the humble temmoku bowls and the spontaneous Cizhou stoneware captivate me.

It is a welcoming sight to visit villages that are still producing needed pots, such as pickle jars whose double rim, filled with water and covered with an inverted bowl, becomes airtight. Huge wine and water containers, usually covered with brown slip glaze, are still produced all over China, as are bricks and roof tiles fired in the "water reduction" method that has been used for 50 centuries. This involves a shallow pool for water on top of the beehive kiln, which allows water to seep through the kiln walls when the firing temperature is reached ($H_2O + C = CO + H_2$). The water in combination with the carbon creates the reducing atmosphere responsible for the ubiquitous gray bricks and tiles seen all over China!

I have been asked: How has your China experience affected your work? The essence of a foreign culture and its art always requires time for me to process, and I have not yet detected any direct or immediate effect. By contrast, my earlier experience with Asian culture, in Japan in the '60s, was very different. It was a stunning discovery and exploration for a receptive, innocent foreigner not too many years out of graduate school. When Kaneshige Toyo, a potter who was a Japanese Living National Treasure, came to Michigan in 1960, he demonstrated with a relaxed attitude and sensitivity to the clay that captivated me and my students. We learned about wood firing and unglazed surfaces as well as about the organic conception of clay. When he invited me to Japan I did not hesitate. It was a splendid opportunity to work in Bizen, an ancient pottery village where time stood still. I was totally immersed in the world of an exotic culture offering a unique pottery tradition and a clay vocabulary that I was eager to accept.

Having digested this first Asian experience, I think I have now established a mature perception, ripened by decades of work. My recent China experience has been immense, and the influences seem elusive, but with the flow of time an unconscious expression may prevail. It is the culmination of years of rejected and accepted experiments that defines my work.

This article was originally published in *Studio Potter* magazine, Summer/Fall 2010 Boundaries/Digital — Vol. 38 No. 2.

Select Works, Projects & Awards

"I think she'll continue as long as she can
pick up a piece of clay."

IAN LEVINE, MARIE'S SON

BORN   April 3, 1928   Seattle, Washington

EDUCATION

BFA, 1954
University of Washington
Seattle, WA

Certificate, 1954
California College of the Arts
Oakland, CA

MFA, 1956
Cranbrook Academy of Art
Bloomfield Hills, MI

Studied with
Kaneshige Toyo, a Japanese Living
    National Treasure
Tokyo, Japan

APPRENTICESHIPS AND RESIDENCIES

2001 Shiwan Ceramic Residency
Shiwan Ceramic Museum
Foshan, Chanchen District
Guangdong, China

Guest Lecturer
2005 Sanbao Ceramic Art Institute
Jingdezhen, China

2007 Fuping International
    Ceramic Residency
FuLe International Ceramic Art
    Museum (FLICAM)
Xi'an, Shaanxi, China

Residency
Kent State University
Kent, OH

PRIMARY WORK EXPERIENCE

1956, 1960 & 1988
Instructor
University of Michigan
Ann Arbor, MI

1963, 1965
Instructor
University of Washington
Seattle, WA

1965, 1967
Professor
Chulalongkorn University
Bangkok, Thailand

1980, 1990
Instructor
College for Creative Studies
Detroit, MI

PERMANENT COLLECTIONS

Musée Ariana
Geneva, Switzerland

Crocker Art Museum
Sacramento, CA

Benaki Museum
Athens, Greece

Latvian National Museum of Art
Riga, Latvia

FuLe International Ceramic
    Art Museum
Xi'an, Shaanxi, China

Icheon World Ceramics Center
Icheon, Gyeonggi, South Korea

Fuping/HAP Pottery International
    Ceramic Workshop and
    Exhibition
Beijing, China

Shiwan Ceramics Museum
Foshan, Guangdong, China

Everson Museum of Art
Syracuse, NY

Detroit Institute of Arts
Detroit, MI

Shigaraki Ceramic Cultural Park
Koka City, Shiga, Japan

The Alfred Ceramic Art Museum
Alfred, NY

Cranbrook Art Museum
Bloomfield Hills, MI

Jingdezhen Ceramic
    Institute Museum
Jiangxi, Fuliang, China

Comerica Bank Corporation
Detroit, MI

Fireplace design for Levitt House
Bloomfield Hills, MI

Mills College Art Museum
Oakland, CA

Dow Automotive Corporation
Auburn Hills, MI

Leningrad Vera Mukhina Higher
    School of Art and Design
St. Petersburg, Russia

Henry Art Museum at University of
    Washington
Seattle, WA

AWARDS

2020 Eminent Artist Award
Kresge Foundation
Troy, MI

2019
Lifetime Artist Achievement
Michigan Ceramic Arts Association

2017 Gold Medal Award
The Scarab Club
Detroit, MI

1998 Asian Cultural Council
    Research Grant
The Rockefeller Foundation
New York, NY

Artist Achievement Award
Michigan Council for Arts and
    Cultural Affairs

International Ceramics Festival
Mino, Japan

Michigan Council for Arts and
    Cultural Affairs

International Ceramic Exposition
Ostend, Belgium

Annual Show Awards
Michigan Potters Association

Syracuse Ceramic National
    Exhibition
Syracuse Museum of Fine Arts
Syracuse, NY

Purchase Award
Smithsonian International
    Exhibition (Smithsonian
    Institution)
Washington DC

Horace Rackham Research Grant
University of Michigan
Ann Arbor, MI

Purchase Award
Joslyn Art Museum
Omaha, NE

SOLO SHOWS

2004
Chapman Friedman Gallery
Louisville, KY

2008
Clay Odyssey
Birmingham Bloomfield Art
    Center Gallery
Birmingham, MI

2006
The Randolph Arts Guild
Asheboro, NC

2007
A joint show

Birmingham Bloomfield Art
    Center Gallery/The Scarab
    Club
Detroit, MI

1997, 1999, 2001, 2003
Shaw Guido Gallery
Pontiac, MI

Habatat Galleries Detroit
Farmington Hills, MI

Sisson Art Gallery
Dearborn, MI

DeWaters Art Center
Flint, MI

1996, 1998
Pewabic Pottery Gallery
Detroit, MI

Downer Art Gallery
Milwaukee, WI

Troy Art Gallery
Troy, MI

Gallery 4 Art Gallery
Detroit, MI

Mi Chou Gallery
New York, NY

University Art Gallery (Central
    Michigan University)
Mt Pleasant, MI

LECTURES, RESIDENCIES & WORKSHOPS

FuLe Artist Residency
Fuping ,Shaanxi, China

Visiting Artist
Haystack Mountain School of
    Crafts
Deer Isle, ME

Visiting Artist
Peters Valley School Of Craft
Layton, NJ

Slide Lecture
Shijiazhuang University
Shijiazhuang, Hebei, China

University of Arizona
Tucson, AZ

Visiting Artist
Kent State University
Kent, OH

Arrowmont Ceramic
    Conference Panel
Gatlinburg, TN

Workshop
University of Louisville
Louisville, KY

RESIDENCY

Shigaraki Ceramic Museum
Koka, Shiga, Japan

Slide Lecture
Asia Institute Crane House
Louisville, KY

Visiting Artist
92Y Ceramics Center
New York, NY

Visiting Artist
Asheboro Ceramic Symposium
Asheboro, NC

Foshan Ceramic Residency
    (Shiwan Ceramic Museum)
Foshan, Guangdong, China

Visiting Artist
Kaneshige Toyo/ Studio
Bizen, Okayama, Japan

Visiting Artist
Tamura Koichi /studio
Sano, Tochigi, Japan

Visiting Artist
University of Iowa
Iowa City, IA

Visiting Artist
Webster University
St. Louis, MO

Visiting Artist
University of Illinois
Springfield, IL

Slide Lecture
Hangzhou China Academy of Art
Hangzhou, Zhejiang, China

Visiting Artist
Georgia State University
Atlanta, GA

Lecture
Detroit Institute of Arts
Detroit, MI

Slide Lecture
Michigan Asian Art Society
Detroit, MI

Invited Panelist
World Conference on Women, 1995
Beijing, China

Our Congratulations

Kresge Arts in Detroit is honored to celebrate Marie Woo as the 2020 Kresge Eminent Artist. Her groundbreaking personal work, including vessels, sculptures, installations, and the creation of her signature and sought-after glazes "Woo Blue" and "Woo Yellow," achieve the often-elusive aspiration that drives many visual artists — honoring tradition while simultaneously pushing a form forward.

Her work as a scholar, preservationist, curator and educator have further influenced, sustained and connected the field of ceramics. Woo's ceramics are of such arresting beauty and intriguing form that the pieces both catch the eye and hold the attention of heart and mind.

Woo has lived an artist's life, including leaps of faith that required leaving behind a seemingly secure future. She stayed true to her chosen materials, the lineage of her craft, and her gift for discovering new paths forward. In doing so, she has pushed the limits of the material, expanded our collective understanding of ceramics as an art form, and exemplified what it means to be a visual artist.

Marie Woo's elevation of earth and clay to shimmering beauty is a reminder of the exquisite nature of our surroundings, and the opportunity to transform the everyday into the extraordinary.

CHRISTINA DE ROOS

DIRECTOR, KRESGE ARTS IN DETROIT

Marie Woo's selection to receive the lifetime achievement award as the 2020 Kresge Eminent Artist for a career spanning more than 70 years is significant as she is the first Kresge Eminent Artist honored for work in ceramics. Always exploring, learning and teaching, her reach is global and intimate. The honor is well deserved.

She has established a robust legacy, sharing her passion as an educator and as a passionate preservationist of nearly extinct Chinese folk pottery, and for having worked to expand awareness and access to the work of others.

Over her career, most of which has been spent in the Detroit area and includes teaching at the College for Creative Studies, University of Michigan and Pewabic Pottery, Marie Woo has become the "potter's potter," inspiring others — peers, students, teachers and the public. She is a technical master and innovator, embracing and expanding traditional responses to clay and more; her work resides in many prominent collections.

The College for Creative Studies is proud to stand with, honor, celebrate and congratulate Marie Woo as the 2020 Kresge Eminent Artist.

DON TUSKI, PHD

PRESIDENT, COLLEGE FOR CREATIVE STUDIES

The Kresge Eminent Artist
Award and Winners

THE 2020 KRESGE EMINENT ARTIST SELECTION COMMITTEE

Marie Woo was named the 2020 recipient of the Kresge Eminent Artist Award by a distinguished group of artists and arts professionals.

Janet Webster Jones Owner-operator of Source Booksellers in Detroit

Laura Mott Curator of Contemporary Art and Design, Cranbrook Art Museum

Nii O. Quarcoopome Curator of African art and head of the department of Oceanic & New World Cultures, Detroit Institute of Arts

Patricia Terry-Ross Harpist, vocalist, educator and 2017 Kresge Eminent Artist

Ralph Valdez Executive Director of the Dearborn Community Arts Council

MaryAnn Wilkinson Executive Director of the Scarab Club

THE KRESGE EMINENT ARTIST AWARD

Established in 2008, the Kresge Eminent Artist Award honors an exceptional literary, fine, film or performing artist whose influential body of work, lifelong professional achievements and proven, continued commitment to the Detroit cultural community are evident. The Kresge Eminent Artist Award celebrates artistic innovation and rewards integrity and depth of vision with the financial support of $50,000. The Kresge Eminent Artist Award is unrestricted and is given annually to an artist who has lived and worked in Wayne, Oakland or Macomb counties for a significant number of years. The Kresge Eminent Artist Award, annual Kresge Artist Fellowships, Gilda Awards, and multiyear grants to arts and cultural organizations in metropolitan Detroit constitute Kresge Arts in Detroit, the foundation's core effort to provide broad support to the regional arts community. The College for Creative Studies administers the Kresge Eminent Artist Award on behalf of The Kresge Foundation.

Complimentary copies of this monograph and others in the Kresge Eminent Artist series are available while supplies last. All monographs are also available for download. Visit **kresge.org** or scan the QR code at left for more information.

PREVIOUS KRESGE EMINENT ARTIST AWARD RECIPIENTS

PATRICK BARBER

Gloria House, 2019

NOAH ELLIOTT MORRISON

Wendell Harrison, 2018

JULIE PINCUS

Patricia Terry-Ross, 2017

JULIE PINCUS

Leni Sinclair, 2016

ELLY STEWART

Ruth Adler Schnee, 2015

MICHELLE ANDONIAN

Bill Rauhauser, 2014

MICHIGAN OPERA THEATRE

David DiChiera, 2013

LON HORWEDEL

Naomi Long Madgett, 2012

PAUL DAVIS

Bill Harris, 2011

JUSTIN MACONOCHIE

Marcus Belgrave, 2009

NICK SOUSANIS

Charles McGee, 2008

ABOUT THE KRESGE FOUNDATION

The Kresge Foundation was founded in 1924 to promote human progress. Today, Kresge fulfills that mission by building and strengthening pathways to opportunity for low-income people in America's cities, seeking to dismantle structural and systemic barriers to equality and justice. Using a full array of grant, loan and other investment tools, Kresge invests more than $160 million annually to foster economic and social change.

PUBLICATION TEAM

Rip Rapson President and CEO

Jennifer Kulczycki Director, External Affairs & Communications

Julie A. Bagley Assistant, External Affairs & Communications

W. Kim Heron Senior Communications Officer, External Affairs & Communications

Alejandro Herrera Graphic Designer, External Affairs & Communications

CREATIVE TEAM

Nichole Christian Creative Director & Editor

Patrick Barber Art Director & Designer

"You can't overwork clay. It naturally dies. But when you learn to leave it alone it has a charm of its own."

Index

This index is sorted letter-by-letter. *Italic* page locators indicate photographs on the page.

A
Adair, James, 15–16
Asian Cultural Council, 58, 94

B
Barringer, Mary, 38–40
Birmingham Art Association, 44
Birmingham Bloomfield Art Center, 16, *45, 50*
Bowl (1991), *71*
Bowl (2006), *79*
Bowls (ca 1981), *69*
   brickmaking, 98–99

C
Carney, Margaret, 57–61
China
   folk pottery and preservation, 14, 26, 32–33, 56, 57–61, *59–60,* 94–99 *95–97*
   kilns, *24, 26,* 58, 94, *95,* 98–99
   modernization, 56, 58, 94, 96
Christian, Nichole, 12–35
Chulalongkorn University, 29
clay
   exposure and training, 22, 44
   historical techniques, 28, *98*
   qualities, and working, 9, 12, 14, 18, 28, 35, 48, 52, 53–54, *54,* 99, 109

Clay Ten (ceramics collective), 33, 48–50
College for Creative Studies, 14, 53, 104
Cranbrook Academy of Art, 22, *24, 28, 40*
creative process and work methods, 9, 12, 14, 16, 18, 28, 30, 41, 43–44, 48, 52, 54, 55. *See also* clay
Crowell, Susan, 58
Cushing, Val, 57
cylinder form, 51
Cylindrical Vase (1965), *67*

D
deRoos, Christina, 104
Detroit, Michigan area
   arts within, 14, 22, 34, 48–50, 52–53, 105
   relocation and home life, 22, 31–32

F
folk pottery
   learning and education, 26, 28, 53, 57, 94
   styles and fashioning, *98*
   Woo preservationism and documentation, 14, 32–33, 56, 57–58, *60,* 61, 94–99, *95–97*
Footed bowl (ca 1958), *65*

G
gender norms, 20
glazes
   China, 98
   examples, *39, 76, 77*
   Woo technique and renown, 24–25, 61
Glick, John, *50*
Griffith, Roberta, 25
Grotell, Maija, 22, 24, 25, 40, *40*

J
Japan
   pottery and influences, 26, 28, 98
   Woo travel and life, *27,* 28–29, 98
Jar (2006), *77*

K
Kaneshige Toyo, 26, 28, 98
kilns
   China, *24, 26,* 58, 94, *95,* 98–99
   home construction and use, 31, *32,* 43–44
Kresge Foundation, 14, 108
Kresge Foundation Eminent Artist Award, 14, 106
   previous recipients, *107*
   Woo (2020), 6, 14–15, 34–35, 48, 61, 104–105, 106

L

Lao Tzu, 26
Levine, Harvey, *19, 27,* 28–29, 31, 43–44
Levine, Ian, 29, 31–32, 33–34, 43
Levine, Leslie. *See* Raymond, Leslie
Li, Jackson, 58
Li Jiansheng, 96
Lumpy Bed (wall installation), *62–63*

M

McBride, Steve, 52–54
metal, 47
Michigan Ceramic Arts Association, 16
Minyao. See folk pottery
Momoyama revival movement, 28
motherhood, 29, 31–32, 43, 44–46

N

natural elements, art processes, 9, 16, *17,* 47

O

Oyobe, Natsu, 58

P

Pewabic Pottery (Detroit, MI), 33, *49,* 52–53, *53*
Phardel, Tom, 48–50, *49, 50*
pickle jars, *59,* 98
Plumer, James, 26, 94
preservationism, ceramics
Chinese folk pottery, 14, 26, 32–33, 56, 57–58, *60,* 61, 94–99, *95–97*
Woo influences and learning, 28, 94

R

Rapson, Rip, 6–7, 14–15
Raymond, Leslie, 31–32, 33, 43–46, *44, 45*
rusty metal, 47

S

Scarab Club Art Gallery, 34
sculptural works, 12, 49–50
Seattle, Washington, 20, 22
Song Dynasty pottery, 26, 57, 94
"The Spirit of Chinese Pottery" (article), 93–99
Stephenson, John, 14, 58
Stephenson, Susanne, 14, 58
Stratton, Mary Chase, 33, 53
studio arts movement, 24
Studio Potter (periodical), 94–99

T

Taoism, 12, 18, 26
Temmoku pottery, 26, 94, 98
Tuski, Don, 105

U

University of Michigan, Ann Arbor
arts programs and exhibitions, 53, 57–58, 61
career, 25–26, 28, 94
Untitled (1989), *70*
Untitled (ca 1992), *73*
Untitled (ca 2000), *75*
Untitled (2010), *81*
Untitled (2014), *85*
Untitled (2016), *91*

V

Vase (ca 1958), *65*
vessel format/tradition, 23, 24, 32, 42, 48, 49

W

Wall piece 2 (2016), *87*
Wall piece 3 (2014), *83*
Wall piece 4 (2016), *88*
Wall piece 5 (2016), *89*
Wall piece 6 (2014), *82*
Wayne State University, 53

Wilkinson, MaryAnn, 24, 32
women artists, 22, 24, 38, 40, 46, 53
Woo, Henry, 20
Woo, Jushi, 20, 21
Woo, Mabel, 20, 21
Woo, Marie
artistic techniques and identities, 6–7, 16, 24–25, *39,* 61
artist's statement, 9
awards, 6, 14–16, 34–35, 48, 61, 101, 104–105, 106
biography, 20–21, 28–29, 31–32, 43, 100
career, 6, 12–15, 24–26, 29, 31–35, 44, 94, 96, 99, 100–103, 105
creative/work processes, 9, 12, 14, 16, 18, 28, 30, 41, 43–44, 48, 52, 54, 55
education and training, 7, 21, 22, 24, 25, 26, 28, 40, 94, 99, 100
exhibitions and collections, 14, 16, 32, 34, *45,* 49–50, *50,* 57–58, 61, 101, 102
influence of, 15, 24–25, 38–40, 46, 52, 104, 105
influences on, 22, 24, 25, 26, 28, 38, 40, 99
personality/descriptions, 12, 16, 18, 25, 33–34, 38, 44, 52, 54, 58, 61
photographs, personal, *15, 19, 27, 29, 30, 32, 34, 45, 49, 50, 53, 54*
photographs, works, *13, 17, 34, 39, 41–42, 44, 45, 47, 50, 51, 54, 55, 62–91*
"The Spirit of Chinese Pottery" (article), 93–99

Z

Zirbes, Georgette, 58

Wonder and Flow

Requests for additional copies of this book, or permission to reproduce material from this work, should be sent to:

The Kresge Foundation

3215 W. Big Beaver Rd.
Troy, Michigan 48084
media@kresge.org

Design and production

Patrick Barber Book design, typography, calligraphy
Katy Balcer Indexer
Alex Cruden Copyeditor

Typeset in Turnip (DJR) and Benton Sans
    (Font Bureau)
Printed and bound in Michigan by KTD Print

The creative team wishes to thank the galleries, museums, universities, photographers, and other art lovers and patrons who worked with us throughout this unpredictable year to gather materials for this book. It is thanks to you that we are able to share such a layered representation of a true ceramic visionary.

Our deepest gratitude also to Ian Levine, Leslie Raymond, and, of course, to Marie Woo, for the many ways you generously traveled back in time to help us capture the pieces of your one remarkable life.

Photography

Unless otherwise noted, photos used throughout this monograph are from the personal collection of Marie Woo. Every effort has been made to locate and credit the holders of copyrighted materials.

Photography credits by photographer

Askew, Richard G. Page 40
Barber, Patrick Front cover, pages 5, 8, 10, 23, 34, 36, 41, 42, 45 (right), 47, 55, 62
Kirkland, Erin Back cover, frontispiece, pages 29, 51, 60 (bottom)
Walker, Haakim Pages 13, 73, 75, 77, 79, 81–83, 85, 87–89, 91
Neese, Dale Page 98
VanGelderen, Annie Page 50

Photography rights information by page

40 Cranbrook Historic Photograph Collection (#4855) Courtesy of Cranbrook Archives, Cranbrook Center for Collections and Research
45 (left) Courtesy of Leslie Raymond
49, 53 Courtesy of Pewabic Pottery/Anne Dennis
65, 71 Courtesy of Alfred Ceramic Art Museum
67 Courtesy of Mills College Art Museum
69 DIA Research Library & Archives Photography Collection—color slides subseries/Michigan Artists 1980–81
70 Courtesy of Detroit Institute of the Arts
79 Courtesy of University of Michigan Museum of Art

ISBN 978-1-7328601-2-4